Where Is Texas?

Where Is Texas?

by Annette Whipple

illustrated by Ted Hammond

Penguin Workshop

Dedicated to all the readers
who celebrate curiosity—AW

PENGUIN WORKSHOP
An imprint of Penguin Random House LLC
1745 Broadway, New York, NY 10019
penguinrandomhouse.com

Designed and Produced by Dinardo Design, LLC.

Library of Congress Cataloging-in-Publication Data is available.

First published in the United States of America by Penguin Workshop, 2025

Manufactured in the United States of America
CJKW

ISBN 9798217051311 (paperback)
10 9 8 7 6 5 4 3 2 1

ISBN 9798217051328 (library binding)
10 9 8 7 6 5 4 3 2 1

The authorized representative in the EU for product safety and compliance is
Penguin Random House Ireland, Morrison Chambers, 32 Nassau Street,
Dublin D02 YH68, Ireland, https://eu-contact.penguin.ie.

Contents

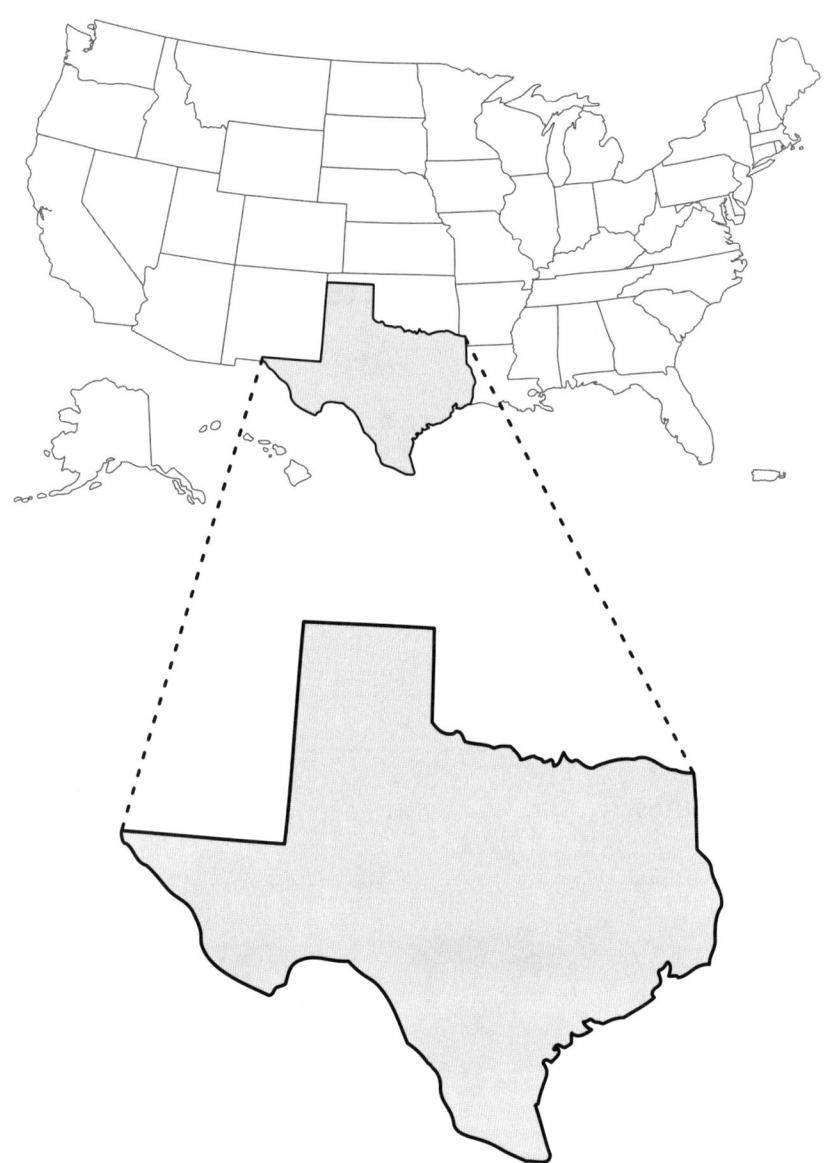

Where Is Texas?

Pattillo Higgins knew Spindletop Hill near Beaumont, Texas, like the back of his hand. In 1900, he'd been drilling for oil for years with no results. People in Beaumont were starting to call him a fool. Higgins knew that if he struck oil, it would all be worth it. He'd be rich.

Finally, on January 10, 1901, a team tried again. First, wet mud bubbled from the thousand-foot hole they had made in the ground. Then, suddenly, oil sprayed to the sky—more than 150 feet in the air! It took over a week to control the huge amount of oil spraying from the ground.

The oil drilling had been successful at last, but Pattillo Higgins wasn't there. He'd been forced out of Spindletop Hill by others looking for oil. It was the beginning of a new chapter in Texas history.

CHAPTER 1
Texas Land and Environment

A familiar saying goes, "Everything is bigger in Texas." That's because everything *is* bigger in Texas. The state is larger than most countries and covers more than 268,000 square miles. New York, Mississippi, and Ohio combined would cover about half of Texas!

Located in the southwest region of the United States, Texas borders the states of New Mexico, Oklahoma, Arkansas, and Louisiana, as well as the country of Mexico. Movies and television often show Texas as flat and dry. Some parts are flat and dry, but Texas also has forests, wetlands, beaches, and prairies. Its highest mountain, Guadalupe Peak, rises out of a desert to reach over 8,700 feet. Scientists have named Texas one of the states with the most diverse kinds of plant and animal life.

Deep beneath the plains, forests, deserts, and mountains, the earth holds information about prehistoric Texas. Scientists think that millions of years ago, shallow saltwater seas covered the land. As the seas dried up, they left behind salt and sediment—sand, rocks, and even once-living sea creatures. Over many thousands of years, these remains became fossils. Later, heavy rock buried the sediment along with lots of salt. The sediment didn't move much, but the salt did. As the rocks pushed down, salt moved up toward the earth's surface in long, skinny columns called salt domes. They could be over a mile tall—and all

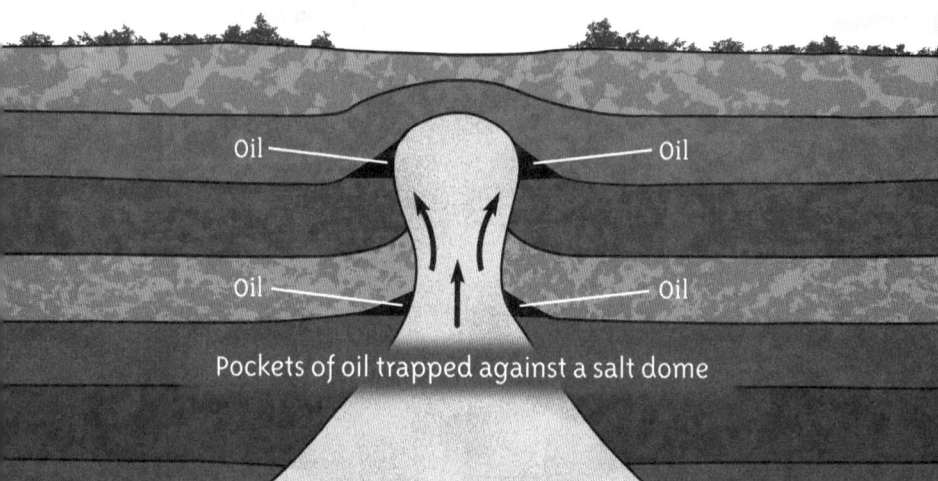

Pockets of oil trapped against a salt dome

underground! Salt domes create pockets that act like storage tanks. When the ancient sediment and fossils decompose (or rot) and create gas or oil, the salt domes trap it. On the earth's surface, salt domes can look like small hills.

Today, the Rio Grande forms the southern border of Texas and the border between the United States and Mexico. It is one of the longest

rivers in North America at about 1,900 miles. Its name means "big river" in Spanish. The Rio Grande's banks and beaches provide a home for hundreds of kinds of butterflies, including several species that don't live anywhere else in the country. More than 1,000 species of plants also live along the river.

Texas's lakes, rivers, swamps, and wetlands

provide habitats (places to live) for animals like river otters, snapping turtles, and water moccasins (a species of snake with a poisonous bite). More species of birds live in Texas than in any other state. About five million migrating birds stop in the wetlands of Texas on their journeys each year. Ruby-throated hummingbirds, for instance, usually arrive in west and south Texas in the fall and build nests out of items from grass to spiderwebs!

Rainfall can be just eight inches a year in the deserts of west Texas. Yucca plants, creosote bushes, and cacti thrive alongside nocturnal animals like coyotes, scorpions, geckos, and bats in this dry climate. Animals rest during the hottest part of the day and look for food at night when temperatures are cooler. Although the desert can sometimes appear empty, many plants and animals live in its harsh conditions.

In East Texas, about sixty million acres of

forest, including the Piney Woods, provide homes to animals like squirrels, cottonmouth snakes, and opossums. Prairies in northern and east-central Texas grow tall grasses and shrubs. Mockingbirds and Texas bluebonnet flowers live on the prairies.

Indigenous peoples—possibly as many as fifty different groups at various times—have lived in what we now call Texas for thousands of years. About seven thousand years ago, the Pueblo (which means village) people created villages and farmed along the Rio Grande.

Other nations like the Karankawa (say: Kuh-run-KA-wah) lived in settlements along the Gulf Coast and ate oysters and fish. Many still live on the same lands today.

Beginning about 800 CE, the Caddo Nation grew squash, beans, and maize in their villages. They traveled for trade, including to the Great Lakes, where they could get copper. The Caddo's family-based groups, called bands, lived in large farming villages and built mounds as temples and homes of important people. Mounds were also used as tombs. Some of the Caddo's large mounds are still visible today.

Christopher Columbus was an Italian explorer who became famous in the 1400s. He was paid

by Spain to go to the American continents. Columbus is remembered for telling the people of Europe about a "new" part of the world as well as his violent efforts to control the land and people he met.

After Christopher Columbus's trip to the Americas in 1492, Spain wanted to explore and

claim more land there. They also hoped to find resources, like gold. Indigenous nations shared the land they had called home for thousands of years with newcomers from Europe. Sometimes they were willing, and sometimes they were forced.

The Apache (say: uh-PACH-ee) and Comanche (say: cuh-MAN-chee) Nations lived on the southern plains. The Comanche Nation arrived in Texas in the 1700s. The Apache Nation had come about a hundred years earlier.

Known for their skill with horses, both nations used bison (the very large mammal also called buffalo) meat for food and hides (skins) for clothing and tents. As nomadic nations, they did not have permanent settlements but moved from place to place. The Apache and Comanche Nations sometimes went to war with each other and other groups, especially over territory.

The name of Texas likely came from the Caddo

greeting "Tay-yas, tay-yas." Meaning *friends*, it was used when Caddo people met Spanish settlers who had arrived in their lands. But things weren't friendly between the Indigenous nations and European settlers for long.

CHAPTER 2
Texas First People and State Origins

In 1519, Alonzo Álvarez de Pineda led a Spanish expedition through the waters we now call the Gulf of Mexico. His group created the first European map of the coastline. Another Spanish explorer crossed the Rio Grande in 1598.

None of the explorers found the treasure they sought, but they did claim the land for Spain. They wanted to colonize the land, or to use its natural resources like crops, lumber, and precious metals like silver and gold to enrich their home nations.

Europeans, mostly from France and Spain, traded with the Caddo and other Indigenous nations. While the Spanish and French fought for the right to colonize the land, Indigenous nations fought to protect the places where they lived. European contact led to extreme hardship for the Indigenous nations. Between 1646 and 1816, the Caddo Nation's population alone dropped by 95 percent due to European diseases and violence.

Mexico became a Spanish colony, and Texas was part of Mexico. Spain ruled Texas from 1690 to 1821. (During that time, to the north and east, the United States won its independence from England.)

The Spanish built churches called missions and homes for soldiers called presidios (say: pri-SEE-dee-ohz). These large buildings with thick walls protected the people inside them as well as nearby settlements. Spain was a Catholic country, a part of the Christian church, and the missions attempted to spread Catholicism.

The Spanish used the missions to influence nearby Indigenous nations to speak and act like them. They also attempted to form relationships

with Indigenous communities. In some cases, they tried to force Indigenous groups like the Karankawa people to live at the missions. Some Indigenous people learned about the Spanish culture, faith, and farming style, all of which were very different from their own traditions. The Karankawa Nation and other Indigenous groups didn't want to be part of the missions. Sometimes the missions were unsuccessful and abandoned.

Presidios were like missions without the religious focus. Spanish soldiers often lived there and patrolled nearby settlements to protect against other nations. Presidios and missions were symbols of Spain's power and wealth. They helped them take and defend land.

By the 1800s, Mexico had been a Spanish colony for hundreds of years. Spain treated Mexican people poorly, though, so they resented their leadership. Mexico, with the help of Texas, rebelled against Spain and became independent in 1821.

Texas was home to people from many places and cultures. Indigenous groups had lived there for thousands of years. People from Africa and their descendants were in Texas because they had been enslaved and brought there to work.

A mix of people who had lived or traveled in other parts of Mexico arrived. People came from European countries like Germany, Poland, and Sweden. Pioneers also came to Texas from the east, where the United States was a young country.

Over time, some people living in Texas thought Mexico made too many laws. Many of them were immigrants from the United States. They didn't like that the Mexican government tried to stop more United States immigrants from moving to Texas, and they didn't want to pay high taxes. They especially didn't like that Mexico wanted to end slavery in Texas in 1829.

Some of the people who came to Texas from the United States were cotton farmers with enslaved people working for them. During this time, the United States economy and many large farms, called plantations, used the labor of enslaved adults and children. Slavery was still legal in the United States. Many enslavers in Texas didn't want to stop even though Mexico outlawed slavery.

In 1835, Texans decided to create their own temporary government. After all, they were the size of some other countries! They needed someone to be in charge. They chose Sam Houston to command the militia—a volunteer army—just in case it was needed. Tension grew between Texas and the Mexican government.

Mexico sent an army to the town of Gonzales, Texas, in the fall of 1835. The army wanted to take a cannon out of the town. The Mexican government gave it to the town for its protection in 1831. Now they wanted it back. The residents of Gonzales refused to give it to the Mexican soldiers. In fact, the people put out a sign for when the soldiers arrived that said, "Come and take it." With that, the Texas Revolution began.

In the end, they didn't wait for the army to arrive in Gonzales. Instead, they surprised the Mexican army in the town of Goliad. The Mexicans retreated to San Antonio but were soon ready to attack again. Nearly two hundred Texas troops moved into a mission called the Alamo to fend off as many as five thousand Mexican soldiers. Sam Houston's small army, including legendary figure Davy Crockett, resisted for two weeks before finally admitting they had lost. People like Crockett became legends when they died there.

On April 21, 1836, Sam Houston led an attack on Mexican troops at the San Jacinto River. They cried out, "Remember the Alamo!" Taken

by surprise, many Mexican troops ran away. Other Mexican soldiers were captured, seriously injured, or killed. Texas won the battle in eighteen minutes! The war was over. Texas declared their independence from Mexico and became a nation called the Texas Republic in 1836.

People in Texas elected Sam Houston their first president. Being an independent country was difficult, though. They were in debt from the war against Mexico and didn't have enough money to defend themselves from Mexican and Indigenous groups fighting over their land. Eventually, Texas leaders asked the United States to take over the national government. The United States would protect Texas and pay their debts. After just ten years as its own country, Texas became part of the United States in December 1845. It was the twenty-eighth state.

The United States and Mexico continued to fight over land in the west from 1846 to 1848. Finally, the Mexican-American War ended when the United States agreed to pay Mexico $15 million for 500,000 square miles of land from the Rio Grande to the Pacific Ocean.

The late 1800s brought more Europeans and Americans to Texas. At the same time, the United States government forced the Caddo, Comanche, and other Indigenous nations to move onto reservations (land the government set aside for them to live on). Many Indigenous people had to leave the state. They were forced not only to give up their homes and land, but to end important cultural and religious traditions.

The reservations were supposed to belong to the Indigenous nations, but the United States government often moved nations from one territory to another. Land was taken away and given to settlers. As Indigenous nations were forced off their lands, more American and European settlers took over.

In Texas (and across the South), growing and harvesting cotton was the base of the economy. Plantation owners were successful because they didn't pay the enslaved people who grew and harvested the cotton. Many people in Texas didn't like it when the United States elected Abraham Lincoln, who opposed slavery, as president.

Other Southern states decided to secede, or

leave, the United States and continue allowing slavery. They formed their own country called the Confederate States of America. Texas joined the Confederacy in 1861. During the Civil War, Texas fought for the South and lost. The Union won the Civil War in 1865, and slavery was abolished (outlawed). In 1870, Texas was readmitted to the United States.

After the Civil War, a period of rebuilding began. In addition to repairing businesses and farms, Texas society needed to change. Slavery had officially ended, but new restrictions for Black, Hispanic (people from Spanish-speaking nations), and other people of color limited their rights. Racism and violence continued.

In Texas's cotton fields, the forced labor of enslaved people was replaced with a system called sharecropping. Some sharecroppers were immigrants from Europe or Mexico. Many were formerly enslaved Black people. Sharecroppers picked cotton and other crops and earned a small amount of money for each pound or basket collected. The money wasn't paid regularly. Sometimes it wasn't paid at all. Their work conditions were very poor (and often not too different from slavery).

This system intentionally kept sharecroppers poor. With hundreds of families working on most plantations, the landowners were the only ones who benefitted. Whole families, including small children, worked in the fields to gather crops. Often sharecroppers' children couldn't attend school because they had to work.

Texas had another key element to its farms: cattle. Cattle are large animals raised for their milk or meat. One kind of cattle called Texas longhorns grew in importance after the Civil War. Ranchers and cowboys moved the cattle over long distances on the way to railroads. Then the cattle were sold and transported across the country.

What Is Juneteenth?

The Confederate general Robert E. Lee surrendered on April 9, 1865. Finally, the Civil War was coming to an end. Enslaved people had been proclaimed free by President Lincoln, and now the Southern states would have to follow his word.

Since enslaved people didn't always have access to news and information, not everyone knew that slavery had become illegal. White enslavers in Texas did not share the news. General Gordon Granger and about two thousand Union troops arrived in Galveston, Texas, on June 19, 1865. The soldiers ordered emancipation of the enslaved people. That meant 250,000 Black people in Texas finally knew slavery had ended in the South.

This day continues to be celebrated each year and came to be called "Juneteenth." June 19 is now a national holiday.

As railroads became more common throughout the state, they provided a fast and cheap way to transport cattle and cotton. While ranching and cotton continued to be a way of life in Texas, a big discovery in 1901 changed things: oil.

CHAPTER 3
Growth and Development of Texas

Over time and with high pressure, once-living things like plants change into the fossil fuel we call oil. People in Texas have used oil for centuries. Small amounts would sometimes leak out of the ground's surface.

Indigenous nations near the Gulf Coast used oil long before the first Europeans arrived. European explorers waterproofed their boats with oil. In the 1800s, people used it for fuel and lamps.

In the late 1800s, Texans built oil wells and drilled into the ground to bring oil to the surface. By 1898, Texas had its first oil refinery, where crude oil (straight from the well) was "refined" and changed into products people could use.

There was a need for refined oil all over the world, especially for fuel.

On January 10, 1901, a group drilled for oil on Spindletop Hill near Beaumont, Texas. They hit a gushing geyser, or a high-pressure spout, that blew oil over 150 feet high. The oil's pressure was so strong that it took nine days to get the geyser under control. Spindletop produced close to 100,000 barrels of oil a day. That was more than all the other oil wells in the country put together!

In 1900, the state of Texas produced around 836,000 barrels of oil. In 1902, Spindletop alone produced more than seventeen million barrels of oil. The modern oil industry was born.

Lots of people moved to Texas for work related to the new oil industry. Beaumont's population grew to fifty thousand in a few months. Spindletop's success caused people to drill for oil throughout the state. More refineries were built. The oil boom meant jobs and money for Texas.

Some people bought and sold land that was worth more because of the oil under its surface. Many worked in oil drilling and refining. Oil drilling in Texas continued for decades.

The oil boom brought excitement and wealth to Texas. Many small towns grew into cities. Oil companies were formed. With more money in the state, new roads, towns, and railroads were built.

But in the early 1900s, despite the oil boom, many rural areas still didn't have electricity. In factories and on farms, children often worked instead of attending school. Segregation and discrimination against Black people and Mexican Americans in Texas continued.

Farming and oil dominated Texas in the early 1900s. Then came the stock market crash of 1929 and the Great Depression. During this period of economic crisis, many businesses didn't have enough money to pay employees. People were out of work and unable to afford food or medical care.

In the 1930s, a major drought (an extended period without rain) hit the southern plains region of the United States, including Texas. It lasted for years and was called the Dust Bowl. High winds blew dry soil away. Dust storms blocked the sun for hours at a time. The worst of these storms, called Black Sunday, spread east from Oklahoma and blew as much as three million tons of soil into the air. During the Dust Bowl years, the thirsty land only produced a fraction of the crops it previously grew. This meant less food and money for farmers and their families, and less food for the rest of the country as well.

When World War II began in the 1940s, war-related industries provided much-needed jobs. Many parts of Texas provided ideal locations for factories because of their abundant land, oil, and coastline near the Gulf of Mexico. Products manufactured there could easily be shipped to other countries. More people moved from rural Texas to cities in order to work in factories. Military bases also brought more than a million troops to Texas.

Although these jobs helped Texans, many laws and practices still favored white people. Black, Hispanic, and Latino people (people from Latin America or whose ancestors are from Latin America) were often discriminated against. After the war, unfair laws prevented many of these groups from using public spaces like hospitals, parks, theaters, and schools. They endured racism and segregation.

These groups wanted change in Texas in a lot of areas, but mainly in voting and education. They wanted access to good schools for children and for their communities to be represented in political office. Following World War II, people joined activists like Texas civil rights leaders

A. Maceo Smith (an educator and businessman) and Carter Wesley (an attorney), and national leaders like Supreme Court Justice Thurgood Marshall, to demand equality.

Some of the change that people demanded began with city and state governments. Henry B. González, the son of Mexican immigrants, was born in San Antonio, Texas, and grew up speaking Spanish. In 1956, he became the first Mexican American elected to the Texas state senate, and in 1961, he became the first Mexican American elected from Texas to the United States House of Representatives. He, along with many others, worked to stop legal segregation in Texas.

Henry B. González

CHAPTER 4
The Making of Modern Texas

Austin has been the capital of Texas since 1839, and the state government is still based there. The first capitol was a log cabin. The second, a limestone building constructed in 1853, caught fire in 1881 and was replaced by the current capitol, which took seven years to build and was dedicated in 1888. The capitol building stands more than fourteen feet taller than the United States Capitol building in Washington, DC.

More than five hundred thousand people living in Texas identify as having Native American heritage. They come from various nations and many work to preserve and remember their ancestors' traditions and languages.

Texas's location on the Mexican border along

with its diverse population help shape its unique culture. Spanish is spoken in one out of five homes.

Ranching and farming continue to be important. Cowboys still work in Texas—and that's no surprise, since the state leads the country in the number of farms and ranches. Texas leads the way in raising cattle, sheep, and goats, as well as growing cotton.

Traditions are big in Texas. People of all ages—in both cities and rural areas—embrace farm and ranch culture by wearing cowboy hats and boots. Many consider high school football as more than just a sport. It celebrates athletic competition and camaraderie in communities across the state. The excitement continues with college and professional football. Rodeos entertain crowds while displaying the skills of cowboys and cowgirls, which are often first learned on farms and ranches.

Ropin' and Ridin' Rodeos

Rodeo traditions began with Mexican ranch hands in the early 1800s. The sport got its name from the Spanish word *rodear* which means to round up—how cowboys would gather cattle or horses and move them. Nearby ranches competed against one another to show off their skills. The cowboys showcased their talents at racing horses, riding bulls, and roping cattle in competitions.

Soon crowds formed to watch. In party-like atmospheres, audiences cheered on the bold and brave cowboys. Competitors came from various backgrounds and included people of Black, Spanish, Mexican, and Indigenous ancestry.

One popular Texas cowboy, Willie "Bill" Picket of the late 1800s and early 1900s, became famous for how he wrestled cattle to the ground. Picket toured with the famous Buffalo Bill's Wild West shows and later became one of the first Black actors in Hollywood.

In today's rodeos, cowboys and cowgirls still take turns showing their roping and riding skills in timed events. Each event requires an athlete to have unique skills. One event is a wild ride that lasts for eight seconds while an untamed horse or bull tries to buck the rider off! Hooves and horns sometimes injure the athletes in this dangerous sport. To protect the cowboys and cowgirls, bullfighters try to distract angry animals away from the riders.

In 1997, rodeo became the official sport of Texas. People of all ages and backgrounds compete. Even more watch the entertainment. For today's cowboys and cowgirls, it's more than a sport. It's a lifestyle.

Even theme parks celebrate history in Texas! Six Flags Over Texas is an amusement park which opened in 1961 and is named after the six governments that have governed the land. The park offers thrill rides for visitors. It was the first of several dozen Six Flags theme parks around the world.

Texas is known for its great food, influenced by different cultures. "Tex-Mex" is a food style which originated in Texas. Some say Tex-Mex-style food is a blend of Mexican, Spanish, and Indigenous foods. Another popular style of cooking is barbecue, where meat is cooked slowly with smoke. Restaurant and home chefs are passionate about preparing meat in their favorite barbecue style.

Oil continues to be an important industry in Texas. While the drilling and refining of oil in Texas has created economic opportunity for the state, it has also caused problems, like the

loss of wildlife habitats. When oil is used, gases are released into the earth's atmosphere, which scientists now know worsens climate change. More research and new technologies are helping Texas to explore different sources of energy. Solar and wind farms create clean energy sources from the sun and wind. Texas also has thriving technology and aeronautics industries, with NASA (National

Aeronautics and Space Administration) located in Houston and technology companies like Dell computers in the Austin area and Texas Instruments in Dallas.

The preservation of land is important to Texans. Big Bend National Park offers hiking trails, canyons, desert landscapes, and diverse wildlife. The Caverns of Sonora have miles of

tunnels that open into underground caverns. More than three thousand caves and sinkholes can be found throughout Texas. Scientists explore caves to study fossils of unique or extinct animals.

Texans are working to balance the needs of their growing state with the natural environment of the plants and animals that live there. Some of

the wildlife that you can find in Texas includes black bears, coyotes, cougars, and armadillos. But wildlife can be found even in urban areas. Austin is home to the largest urban bat colony in the world! People gather to watch 1.5 million Mexican free-tailed bats emerge from the Congress Avenue Bridge at dusk from April through October.

Some urban areas also offer beautiful scenery. Residents and visitors in San Antonio explore canals, bridges, restaurants, and beautiful landscaping along a historic part of the city called the Riverwalk. In the same city, history comes alive at the Alamo museum, which highlights the 1836 battle during which outnumbered Texans attempted to hold off the Mexican army during the Texas Revolution.

Texas is always changing and adapting. The people of Texas remember the past and look forward to a big future—because everything is bigger in Texas!

Texas at a Glance

Statehood: 1845

Nickname: The Lone Star State

Abbreviation: TX

State Motto: Friendship

State Tree: Pecan

State Large Mammal: Longhorn

State Small Mammal: Armadillo

Capital: Austin

Size: 268,596 square miles

Population: More than 31 million

Famous People from Texas:

Beyoncé Knowles-Carter
(musician), Kelly Clarkson
(musician), Selena Quintanilla
Pérez (musician), Shaquille
O'Neal (basketball player),
Cruz Ortiz (artist)

Austin

State flag

State bird
Mockingbird

State flower
Bluebonnet

FUN FACT:
There are more than 125 million
acres of farmland in Texas!

Timeline of Texas

800	The Caddo people build settlements with mounds
1519	The first map of Texas is created by Spanish explorers
1821	Mexico wins its independence from Spain
1835	The Texas Revolution begins
1836	Texas wins its independence from Mexico and becomes an independent nation
1839	Austin becomes capital of Texas
1845	Texas becomes the twenty-eighth state in the United States
1848	The Mexican-American War ends
1861	Texas joins the Confederate States of America
1865	The Civil War ends
1870	Texas is readmitted to the United States
1901	Oil is struck at Spindletop Hill
1956	Mexican American politician Henry B. González elected to the Texas state senate
1961	First Six Flags amusement park opens
2024	Texas has more than sixteen thousand wind turbines—more than any other state

Timeline of the World

800	— Charlemagne crowned Holy Roman Emperor
1504	— Michelangelo completes his marble sculpture *David*
1607	— Jamestown founded in the colony of Virginia
1718	— City of New Orleans is founded
1775	— The Revolutionary War begins in Lexington and Concord, Massachusetts
1876	— Alexander Graham Bell invents the telephone
1903	— Wilbur and Orville Wright invent and fly the first airplane
1914	— The Panama Canal is completed, connecting the Atlantic and Pacific Oceans
1939	— World War II begins
1969	— Neil Armstrong is the first person to walk on the moon
1991	— The World Wide Web is invented
2019	— The spread of COVID-19 gives rise to a global pandemic
2024	— About fifteen thousand Paralympic and Olympic athletes compete in the Summer Olympics and Paralympics hosted in Paris, France

Bibliography

*Books for young readers

*Forest, Christopher. *Texas Revolution*. Minneapolis, MN: Jump!, 2021.

*Jewel, Kirsti. *What Is Juneteenth?* New York: Penguin Workshop, 2022.

*Pollack, Pam, and Meg Belviso. *What Was the Alamo?* New York: Penguin Workshop, 2013.

Rhodes, Andy. *Texas*. Moon Travel, 2020.

Websites

Texas Beyond History: texasbeyondhistory.net/

Texas Our Texas: texasourtexas.texaspbs.org/

The Story of Texas: www.thestoryoftexas.com/

Texas Parks & Wildlife: tpwd.texas.gov/

Texas State Historical Association: tshaonline.org/home

Texas State Preservation Board: tspb.texas.gov/